D0611773

<u>Testimonials</u>

"She has not spent the past 33 years being a victim. Far from it. Right at the start, a nurse at Bellevue told her, 'You have five minutes out of every day to feel sorry for yourself. The rest of the time you've got to get up and do something.'"

— Clyde Haberman, *The New York Times*

"Sidney Meyer, who is manager of the cabaret where Renee will perform, said that "there are two things I respect in this woman. One is her musical ability. The other is her spirit. She will go far because she is talented and a hard worker."

— Dennis Duggan, *Newsday*

"Her life changed in a split second," observes occupational therapist Pat Casler, "but that wasn't going to stop her." Nor was it going to rob her of her considerable store of compassion. "There is always an area within yourself that you can develop and give to other people," she says.

— Arlene Gottfried, *People Magazine*

"She was eating yogurt with her left hand, a small tribute to the years of therapy that transferred such skills from her right side to her left. "It's a question of concentrating not on what you've lost but on what you've been lucky enough to keep," said Dr. William Shaw, an Associate Professor at New York University Medical Center and Head of Plastic Surgery at Bellevue Hospital.

— Lisa Wolfe, *The New York Times*

"Katz's lovely lyric soprano vocals are one of cabaret's best-kept secrets, and the secret should get out soon – her handling of a variety of numbers are just beautiful to behold. She brings class and great style to anything she decides to sing."

— Andrew Martin, *CAB Magazine*

"Clearly some standouts demand individual mention. These include Renee Katz's beautifully phrased "On My Way to You.""

— John Hoglund, *New York Native*

"She brought Stephen Schwartz's "Meadowlark" to new heights, while her coverage of Maury Yeston's "December Snow," Blitzstein's "I Wish it So," and LeRoy Anderson/Walter Kerr's "I Never Know When to Say When"- proves her taste in music. She's a find!"

— MaryAnn Lopinto, *CAB Magazine*

"And then there's the music. It never stopped. Maybe it no longer flows on the piano or the flute, but she has a voice, put to sweet use."

— Clyde Haberman, *The New York Times*

"Her name will be in bright lights one of these days, and the room will be so full they'll have to put the rope up, standing room only, sorry. Ladies and Gentleman, Renee Katz."

— Dennis Duggan, *Newsday*

NEVER
BEEN GONE

...*A Journey of Possibilities*

By Renee Katz

Deluxe Set includes:
Inspired Poetry Collection
&
Her Debut Vocal Album
Never Been Gone

∞ INFINITY
PUBLISHING

Cover design and graphics by Catherine Wheeler.

Please visit the author's website at **www.reneekatzmusic.com**

ISBN 978-0-7414-9713-0 Paperback
ISBN 978-0-7414-9714-7 eBook
Library of Congress Control Number: 2013911325

Printed in the United States of America

Published February 2014

INFINITY PUBLISHING
1094 New DeHaven Street, Suite 100
West Conshohocken, PA 19428-2713
Toll-free (877) BUY BOOK
Local Phone (610) 941-9999
Fax (610) 941-9959
Info@buybooksontheweb.com
www.buybooksontheweb.com

ACKNOWLEDGEMENT

I would like to express a major heartfelt thank you to Lorraine Danza, Christopher Marlowe, Leigh Angel, Jowill Woodman, Anthony Lombardi, and to my soul-mate Barry Packer, for their expertise and unwavering belief in this project. I also need to share my most sincere appreciation with those who have been there for me through my journey of healing; including the friends, alumni, faculty, and staff of The High School of Music & Art, The New York Choral Society and The Queens Oratorio Society, Ms. Martha F. Gladston, Mr. Sidney Meyer and the Manhattan Association of Cabarets and Clubs; the New York City Police Department, the New York City Fire Department, the First Responders, the late Dr. William Shaw, Dr. Daniel Baker, and the entire microsurgery team at Bellevue Hospital, the late Dr. Howard A. Rusk and the Rusk Institute of Rehabilitation Medicine, the NYU Langone Medical Center, Patricia Casler, OTR, Ellen Ring, RPT; the late Mayor Edward I. Koch and my fellow New Yorkers whose generosity, creativity and compassion all made my rehabilitation successful, and has brought me to where I am today. Lastly, the deepest of gratitude is extended to my parents, son and brother who inspire me on a daily basis with their immeasurable talents and perseverance. Each one of you will remain in my heart, always.

I can see the beauty in the distance and
I want to dance,
I want to dance,
You have given me the chance.

Everything Is Possible by D. Spangler, C. Gore

This book is dedicated to my parents,

Isidore and Rose Katz

&

All Survivors

as well as those cherished people
who inspire us to move forward.

1

INTRODUCTION

Thank you for venturing forth into my experience of the heart. I hope that my words and music will touch your soul, in the same way that so many caring individuals have reached out and touched mine.

"MUSIC STUDENT, 18, LOSES HAND"
New York Post–Late Edition, Thursday, June 7, 1979

My life was all planned out: graduate with honors, attend a top music conservatory, and have a fulfilling career as a concert musician. June 7, 1979, 8:14 AM—My life changed in a split second. I was just 18 days shy of my 18th birthday when, during my early commute to high school, an unknown crazed person pushed me into the path of an oncoming New York City subway train, severing my right hand from my body.

I became an instant celebrity, but not in the way that I had dreamed of.

2

While lying in my hospital bed, a kind nurse named Ethel helped to ground me and see beyond the media glare and the bouts of self-pity that surfaced in the rare quiet moments.

"Good morning, how are you feeling today?" Ethel asked, opening the curtain to reveal the bright sunshine.

"Eh, I've been better," I muttered.

"Renee, listen, you have five minutes out of every day to feel sorry for yourself. The rest of the time you've got to get up and do something," she said, handing me a piece of paper and a pencil. "Now, put this in your left hand and start with the A, B, C's."

"What?" Was she crazy? I couldn't write, especially with my left hand!

"Just try it," she insisted. "You need to be able to use your left hand."

The exercise was boring, and my writing was horrible; but over time, it got better, and I became the person I am today, thanks in part to all that Ethel taught me.

"DISCORDANT NOTE OF EVIL IS HEARD"
New York Daily News, Saturday, June 9, 1979

My daily commute from Flushing, Queens, New York, required me to take a bus and three trains to attend the highly selective High School of Music & Art on West 135th Street in Manhattan. I was a flute major who, for many years, had studied both piano and voice. After practicing diligently, I had earned the second flute chair in the Senior Orchestra. I was also a first soprano in the Senior Choir, as well as a member of the All-City High School Chorus. My love for music came from my mother and grandmother, both accomplished musicians; my ambition to succeed came from my father, a Holocaust survivor and a self-made businessman.

It was the middle of finals week, and I was cramming for my King Lear exam on my way to school when I dozed off on the train and missed my stop. When I woke up, I got off at the next station and waited for a connecting train back to my destination. I was virtually alone on the dimly lit platform at 50th Street and 8th Avenue.

The subway platform smelled of that unique combination of cigarette smoke, urine, and stale beer. Normally bustling with business commuters and students, it was oddly desolate that particular morning, with only a few people milling around and not a cop in sight. I focused on the bright light emerging through the dark tunnel. I could then feel and smell the oncoming tidal wave of burning metal and garbage rising from the tracks below, as the subway train rapidly approached the station. All of a sudden, I felt a very strong, deliberate shove from behind, and a thud as I hit the tracks and the speeding train passed over me.

By some divine intervention, I rolled to the left moving my whole body out of the way, except for my right hand, which was severed at the wrist by the screeching train. People often ask if I passed out at any point during my ordeal. Unfortunately, I never did.

"Mother! Mother!" I screamed. "I've got to go to college! I've got to go to college!"

The conductor, Justo Barreiro, crawled under the train, looking for me. When he finally found me, pinned under one of the cars, he tried to console me. Someone on the platform called EMS and two ambulances arrived—one for me and one for my hand, which the police had packed in ice.

"BELLEVUE'S SAVER TEAM"
New York Daily News, Thursday, June 14, 1979

I was rushed to Bellevue Hospital where a team of specialists in the brand-new field of microsurgery was being assembled. Led by Dr. William Shaw and Dr. Daniel Baker, the team operated on me with the whole city watching. After more than 16 tense hours, they announced that my hand had been reattached with a stabilizing rod, and that they were able to reconnect the major arteries and nerves.

My story was broadcast nationally and internationally and appeared on the front page of every major newspaper in the New York City metropolitan area. My school friends and kind strangers rallied together to give blood. Benefit concerts were arranged to help pay for mounting medical bills. Cards, flowers, and letters streamed in from famous New Yorkers, such as Mayor Koch and violinist Isaac Stern, as well as caring, everyday New Yorkers. Street musicians and artists sent their change, music, and poetry, which I pinned all over my hospital room walls. More than thirty

7

years later, the media continues to follow my story, and I still

receive the token phone call asking for my comments about the

latest subway incident.

"I CAN FEEL, I CAN FEEL, SAYS RENEE"
New York Daily News, Saturday, June 9, 1979

A policeman stood guard outside my hospital room door around

the clock for the entire length of my 37-day stay. Reporters

surrounded my parents' humble home in Queens and the hospital

in Manhattan, trying to score an interview. Photographers hounded

my family, friends, and me whenever we went outside, always

trying to get a picture of the "infamous reattached hand." But I just

smiled and persevered. As the daughter of a Holocaust survivor, I

was used to smiling through discomfort without expressing

emotion. If my dad could do it, so could I.

In a matter of days, I went from being a music student with big

dreams, to a shattered victim of violent crime, to the hope of

8

survival for the whole city. Nobody allowed me to grieve the loss

of my hand, my dreams, or my innocence. Divorcing my first

husband, 13 years later, became the catalyst that brought forth my

grieving process. I needed the chance to grow as an artist and felt

that I would be letting down Nurse Ethel, the medical and

rehabilitation staff, and most importantly myself, by deferring my

dreams any further. After a bad accident, you lose yourself for a

while, but eventually you find your way back home again.

"LIFE IS MUSIC AND THERAPY FOR RENEE KATZ"
New York Times, Monday, January 7, 1980

As I endured multiple follow-up procedures and waited patiently

for the motor and sensory nerves to regenerate, my healing body

and mind craved music. I lugged my casted arm around the

hospital in search for some kindred spirits. I found a piano player,

another singer, and a rickety old piano; together we brought music

back into our lives. Music made me whole again and singing

became my salvation. My vocal teacher insisted on continuing my lessons in the hospital. I felt extremely blessed that I could still sing as it became painfully clear in the weeks ahead, that I would never regain the fine motor coordination necessary to play the flute or piano at the same skill level I had worked so hard to achieve.

I had just been accepted into a five-year program to complete a double degree in Vocal Studies and Early Childhood Education at The New England Conservatory of Music and Tufts University, in Boston. Unfortunately, I needed to revamp my goals in order to stay in New York near my doctors and support system. I continued my hand therapy at The Rusk Institute of Rehabilitation Medicine, where Dr. Howard Rusk, himself, graciously absorbed the entire cost of my years of treatment. During those years, I had the privilege to witness other survivors triumph over their devastating injuries and was truly inspired to rise above mine.

Nothing is more powerful or propels us further than finding our own purpose. Well, there it was, staring me in the face: My

Purpose. After spending a summer as a volunteer intern at The Rusk Institute, I decided to major in occupational therapy and minor in vocal studies at New York University. I wanted to give back to the people who gave me so much.

While I made the choice to pursue occupational therapy as a career, music has remained the core of my soul and no crazed criminal can ever take that away from me. I made the time to study, practice, and perform. To this day, I continue to sing in major choral groups and New York City's cabaret clubs. When I see people moved by my singing, I feel complete. All I ever wanted was to be known for my talent and the messages my music brings—instead of "the girl with re-attached hand." I was honored to be invited to sing at several worthwhile charity events. Former Governor John Lindsay and Barbara Walters asked me to take part in a benefit for Bellevue Hospital Center's AIDS Treatment Facilities. Talk show producers often invited me to participate in survivor shows, where I got to meet other survivors of tragedy—always a humbling experience.

"6 YEARS LATER, A TRIUMPH OVER TRAUMA"
New York Times, Wednesday, August 28, 1985

After graduation, I began my work as a Registered Occupational Therapist with disabled adults and children, which I continue today. My involvement in occupational therapy, both as a patient and therapist, has afforded me some unique insights. I have developed adaptive techniques for work and daily living activities, such as typing, cooking and driving for both myself and my patients. I remember creating finger splints for a pianist and composer with arthritis to decrease her pain and correctly position her fingers on the keyboard. I always try to incorporate music into my patients' therapy—it is a powerful healer—and I gratefully use my personal experience to help others.

During treatment sessions I am often singing; and when a home-care patient has a piano, I have been known to sit right down and play a one-handed piece or one of my mother's compositions with my left hand and the two more mobile fingers of my right hand. I try to show my patients that beauty can still be created within imperfection, and the soul that endures and triumphs over pain has the capacity to surpass what society brands as "perfection". What is most important is to concentrate not on what you've lost, but on what you've been lucky enough to keep! We all have strengths and talents deep within us that we can tap into and develop if we keep our minds and hearts open to the possibility.

Besides my work, two other positive things came from my ordeal: the microsurgery team at Bellevue Hospital was awarded a new grant, enabling the doctors to continue their life-saving work; and new subway safety regulations and additional transit cops were put in place to prevent horrors like mine from happening again.

"SALUTING THE PEOPLE WHO PERSEVERE"
Newsday, Sunday, September 26, 1999

There came the time when I needed to gather up the courage to get back on a New York City subway train. On February 4, 1980, I began my course of study at New York University; and I was determined never to let anything sidetrack me from attaining my goals ever again.

On the first day of my early morning commute to NYU, I anxiously climbed the old familiar stairs to the platform. I kept my eyes fixated to the ground, and my back plastered against the wall of the station. As the train barreled in, I took a deep breath, stepped through the door on wobbly legs, and gratefully took a seat. I quickly noticed a homeless man who was singing and collecting money around the car. His snug, worn-out overcoat could not hide his tattered clothes, nor could his happy, up-tempo song disguise his world-weary eyes. I then noticed, to my utter amazement, that he had a hand injury, too. When he got to me, holding out his cup of change, he noticed my injury and stopped singing for a moment. His cup shook just a bit, as his eyes filled with emotion. I offered him a dollar, but he quietly refused and went on his way, singing as I smiled through my own tears.

What became very clear in that moment is that our compassion for others is what truly connects us all. We are propelled by our passion and purpose to rise above unforeseen challenges. We are all capable of finding and giving love—the greatest purpose of all.

The poetry and music included in this book are set parallel to my life's path, lined with limitless surprises. My passion and my voice remain strong thanks to the love of my family, friends, and countless New Yorkers who would not let my attacker silence my soul. I have been given a gift of perspective that normally comes from a lifetime of living. I know that pain can lead to a greater joy. I have received and strive to give true compassion. I am grateful for all the lessons I have learned in life, and I now welcome any possibility that arises from landing on an unfamiliar shore.

It's taken years for me to come to this place of gratitude. I know how hard it is to face a challenge, to face uncertainty, to face fear…and what it's like to suppress those feelings and pretend everything is okay. I understand why it's so easy to just go through the motions of life.

If you allow yourself to feel those feelings, embrace them, and never erase them, you will be amazed at the journey that awaits you. I continue to embrace life joyfully, grateful to add to the layers of perspective, compassion, and love to my soul.

Please join me.

Profound Impact
(A Tribute to My Father)

After reading Elie Wiesel's book, "Night,"
I thought of my own father's plight
How similar their ordeals must have been
In the early to mid 1940's, when Nazis
      committed incomprehensible sins.
Both boys were born into close-knit, pious
      communities in Transylvania.
Where No Jew at that time could
      escape Hitler's mania.
Both were rounded up and transported via
      cattle car to Auschwitz concentration camp at night.
Upon arrival—separation, "selection"— their mothers,
      baby sisters and brothers incinerated on sight.
Both chosen as workers of this death factory;
      they were only teenagers back then.
Little did they know how this horror
      would transcend
Their lives forever—
My life forever—

A first generation daughter
Trying to rationalize the slaughter
Of half my family not so long ago
Trying to rationalize, why I still don't know
My own father's personal story
So terrifying it truly must be.

And so, my imagination often takes flight
With Elie's memories in "Night," I have been given
      more insight

I now know why my father appears
      always on the run

17

Working, gardening—never resting, even
        at age eighty-one.
The SS would beat them, if their
        work wasn't completed fast
Numbing them into submission, knowing
        each moment could be their last.

I now know why my father must
        have his daily soup and bread.
He equates this meal with life, the only
        one these "walking corpses" were fed.

I now know why my father can't
        express emotion even though he tries.
At King David's tomb in Israel, is the one
        and only time, I've seen him cry.

On that trip we also experienced "Yad Vashem"
The children staring back at me have been
        burned in my soul since then
Could one of them be related to me?
I could be the face staring down at you,
        so easily.

How could God and the world turn a deaf
        ear to Six Million Souls?
Whose collective screams were never heard—
        their stories and dreams never told.

I search for my father, praying this memorial
        in Israel would bring him peace.
Maybe if he could share his story—
        my tortured thoughts would cease
As if they ever could—
I knew they never would—

I finally found my father, staring blankly,
        rushing through it all
Still burdened by so many unknowns,
        I try to stand tall.
Over the years, there are facts I've been
        able to uncover
With each tidbit of knowledge, a glimmer
        of healing is discovered.

I now know I am named for "Regina,"
        the Grandmother I never knew
A mother of five, all young and alive—
        Silenced— just because, they were JEWS.

The Nazis succeeded to "Silence"
        my father…but in a different way.
These atrocities he has born witness to
        need to be told, so future generations
        will not be led astray.

My children will learn from their Grandfather
What terms strength of spirit
        and bravery truly mean
They will learn how my father's life
        epitomizes "The American Dream."

Upon liberation, the Red Cross sent my
        father to Sweden for medical care
My father will never forget the kindness
        and mercy he received there.

Apprenticed to a tailor before the war, my
        father soon returned to his trade.
Arriving in America via Ellis Island, there
        was a new life to be made.

19

He immediately enrolled himself into English class
Reading only American papers, he would learn fast.
Working long hours by day,
Attending college at night,
My father was now a pattern maker, with a
          dream of his own business in plain sight.

His dream became a reality—thriving over
          forty years to date
Investing in real estate wisely, becoming
          wealthy is his hard-earned fate.
Despite his success, my father remains a
          modest, hard-working and generous man.
A staunch supporter of Israel and an
          extremely patriotic American.

His family roots of farming and self-sufficiency
can be seen on his land, surrounding his
          small home in Queens.
Where my son loves to harvest the fruits
and vegetables with Grandpa—they make
          quite a team.

Keeping his family happy, healthy and
          close means everything to him.
Not a moment wasted! That would be a sin.
That's precisely and how urgent I feel
about recording our family's history
          before it's too late.
Dwelling in the past is something
          my father truly hates.

Only happy stories, only happy songs
Let's gloss over it. Never talk about it.
          When things go wrong.

"We must go on, We must smile,
We must endure."

There's one thing, I know for sure—
I must feel, I must <u>not</u> go numb—You'll See

The Nazis will not **SILENCE** me!

A first generation daughter
Trying to rationalize the slaughter
Of half my family, not so long ago.

A Little Would Mean So Much
(A Tribute to My Mother)

A Gypsy hidden behind huge anxious
      soulful eyes.
Pent-up nerves—a passion running deep—
      yet unsatisfied and frustrated.
Made to feel insecure in a society
      unfair to the hearing-impaired;
And from a husband, controlling and
old-fashioned as to what a woman's
      role "should be."

So gentle and giving
So incredibly intelligent
So talented
So incredibly passive on the outside
An undeniable anger seething
      on the inside
My mother doesn't know how to
      complain or change
She accepts what is given to her
And never appears to want more.

Then why does she cry at night?
And why does she pound the piano by day?

Quiet and smiling in social situations
An occasional outburst of her "notorious
      nervous laugh"
Extremely uncomfortable she might say or
      do "the wrong thing"
As people often laugh or are perplexed by her.

Think she doesn't realize this?
Think it hasn't been tough for her?

22

As a child she was diagnosed with
      partial nerve damage in both ears
She was language-delayed as a child
      and taught sign language and lip reading.
Despite the odds, she caught up in
language and graduated high school
      and college with honors.

An occasional story she'll tell of cruel
      kids who poked fun at her hearing aids.
Of contests she should have won—if
      only they would have repeated the question.

Her dream was to become a teacher
But back then people with disabilities
      weren't allowed to teach.
Instead she worked for two years—
      as a bookkeeper.
She left her job to get married
      and quickly had a family
My mother did everything for her
      family and widowed mother.
          Still Does—

She derives some satisfaction through
the lives of her children, her wild
stories of her eccentric Russian family
and from old movies, musicals and
      mystery novels

My mother has an uncanny instinct
For figuring out people's true souls—
      <u>except her own</u>—
She lives her life through and for others
But has never quite found or left
      room for herself in there.

My mother composes and improvises
             her own music—
A mixture of gypsy and folk music
             for piano.
When she plays, it is often louder
             due to her hearing deficit
People don't always take the time
             to listen to her.

Not understanding her inner core and
just how talented and wonderful
             she truly is.

My mother is someone in pain,
             misunderstood for most of her life.
Wishing so much to be noticed and
             respected.
Wanting admiration for her contributions
             and yes, for being a housewife.

A little would mean so much to her—

It always has—That's why I love her so.
I'm so proud of her—

She is the most lovely, gentle
             person I know.

Everything is beautiful and dangerous and possible and new to me. The waves are not my enemies, the wind is now my friend, the road I hated yesterday, I never want to end.

Everything Is Possible by D. Spangler, C. Gore

I believe we are all survivors in one way or the other. Our collective scars, whether visible or hidden, give us all a unique perspective that we can utilize to help heal our imperfect world. I believe this is the greatest catalyst for positive change.

Thank you for sharing the journey with me.

Wildflowers and Daisywishes
(Dedicated to the young victims of the world)

Growing up before your time
You had to, you had no choice
A meadow of Wildflowers and Daisywishes
Plowed down by evil depths of darkness…

Now still miraculously here, like a perennial—
Surviving and growing subtle layers year by year
That makes one see in a slightly different light.

Appreciating what's less visible to others
As time is so precious, and so is love
Always questioning, vulnerable and scared
      -    but with inner core strength.

No use getting down all the time—
'Cause then evil wins, he reigns—'cause
        he's gotten you just where he wants you…

You cannot let that happen
Gather strength from kind others
Shine with a new perspective—
Develop other talents within you—
        no matter how small you think they are.

And fight, and smile, and cry and then
            gather strength…
      And fight and cry and smile again!

      Let others in.
      Live and Love.
      Strive for what's real—and important to
      your soul
           and

Don't forget the Wildflowers and Daisywishes...

Miss Wish Upon a Star

Can't touch her—she'll break
Porcelain Perfection—Flawed—Double take
God, What a shame! (whispers…)
Oh Yes! I remember that name—
Six-year-old child, playing at her feet
Wooden flute in hand, it's destiny they meet
"I could teach you to play, and it's fun too!"
4-feet high, repeats, "Would you like *me* to teach *you*?"

Humor from above
Tears now full of love
Humbling new beginnings within sight
Suspended time, the evolution of life

Wildflowers and Daisywishes—
Silent understanding, in dreams their soul kisses
Look at that smile, man, she even glows
She's turned herself off—she doesn't even know
No time to feel or deal
Her life perfectly mapped out year by year

Growing up without a choice
Music ripped from her soul—her inner voice
Suppress it—Passion must be kept at a distance
Overcome adversity at everyone's insistence

T.V., Parties, Newspapers—Mannequin from afar
She's everybody's, "Miss Wish Upon a Star"
Protect her at all costs—
Why didn't anyone let her grieve her loss?
Why didn't anyone let her feel her fears?
Lost so long, in the pretense years

Until now…

Surrender to who you truly are
Stop being everybody's "Miss Wish Upon a Star"
Light a fuse and pray
I am my own person today…

Someday…

I plan to recapture my Wildflowers
          and Daisywishes
With someone who loves me for me
Someone who has that key to my Chained Intensity
Where is that one special one?
The journey is long but really…
          it's just begun…

Lone Rose

Four roses in a vase
Each by itself—
Yet together enhancing each other's beauty.
I feel these long silhouettes of softness—
Striving to clear my mind's mist.
Yet the petals are falling, choking—
The anger and confusion bind together like a kinetic force—
Ruining the innocence and simplicity of one single rose.
The other three come to the aide of their kin—
But ultimately it must be left alone.
Alone, to get accustomed to its new atmosphere—
To overcome or just live, despite the foreboding force.
So that it can do justice to the God that created it—
To thank the other three roses that enhanced it—
But mainly, to live…and be satisfied with itself.

Chained Intensity

Searching for an answer
Like the "Red Shoes" Dancer
A soul guided by passion
Driven in an uncontrollable fashion

Need to be free
Need to be loved for me
Scared I'll self-destruct
Maybe I am just a selfish fuck

Angry and enraged
An artist in a cage
Sunshine and rainbows
Bursting out of control

Hidden in the torment of the light
If I smile, will it all be alright?
Sing, Sing, Sing
I just can't hurt anybody or anything

An occasional attempt, I take a stand—
Did I really think I could make them understand?
Inhale the pain, that's what my life is about

Chicken-shit risk-taker, 'cause I've been
          filled with self-doubt

So long, Wildflowers and Daisywishes
So long, dreams my soul kisses
Never for me
Strangled in my Chained Intensity—

Out of Touch

Deep down you know it's there
Easier to pretend you don't care
You can laugh, you can walk away
Save it all for another day—

It's the game of "Out of Touch"
Scared to feel, Scared to deal
Listen to your heart and
You might appear "too real"

"Too real" to cry, yell—maybe lose control
Unlock that curtain surrounding your soul
Everyone's fine, status quo—
You say you know, but what do you know?

Do you know what it's like to be near—But not heard?
Do you know how to touch—with your heart?
Maybe you do—but how would I know?
Is there a place to start?

It's the game of "Out of Touch"
Scared to feel, Scared to deal
Listen to your heart and
You might appear "too real"

"Too real" to take the time
To listen, to talk, maybe empathize
To try and feel, what the other feels
Can't we compromise?

Can't our goals somehow "blend"?
We don't have to run or to pretend
I love you and you love me
But we just can't see, what we want to see—

It's the game of "Out of Touch"
Scared to feel, Scared to deal
Listen to your heart and
You might appear "too real"

It's a game of "Out of Touch"
Let's now deal with how we feel
<u>Listen</u> to our hearts, and
we've got a chance
<u>to make it "Real"</u>

A Valentine's Hug of Passionless Regret

Somehow there are tears now
      in your beautiful brown eyes—
Where were they when I
      reached for you?
Why couldn't our tears meet
      before our lives parted?
Why didn't you meet me
      even half way?
And now you say let's
      run away—
Always running away—
Always dreaming of a better life
      to fill *Your* goals—
What about mine?
My goals—my confidence
      suppressed by your insecurity
And *now* you see me—
      with tears in your eyes
Yet you have no way to
      reach my soul—
You were too proud to
      admit we needed help
You let us slip away
A Valentine's Hug of
      passionless regret—
Yes, with tears in your eyes—
      Amazing—
Connected, Yet Unconnected
      Forever…

      My Childhood
      My Innocence

      Now...

Changing—
Growing—

Yet a piece
Always to remain within—
Aching with your pain—
Wishing you knew how to
         Reach Me—

         but mostly
Wishing you knew how
         to reach Yourself

Now…Too late—My First Love
A Valentine's Hug of Passionless Regret

Dedication to the Process

Sometimes love is just not enough, if two people
require different environments, needs, goals to
make them happy.

It is true love, when one recognizes they
cannot change their partner's goals and aspirations
to fit their own needs.

When one attempts to change the other,
resentment can only abound.

If you choke a dream, you are attempting to
rip away the core essence of what makes
the person unique—

Without this core essence, the person feels
empty and incomplete.

When a person's dream is considered
unworthy in the eyes of someone they care for,
it fills them with self-doubt, reducing their courage
and aspiration to pursue their dream.

Life is rejoicing in each other's attempt
to attain growth and dreams, and respecting
the core essence of what makes
           each person unique.

On My Own the Way It Has to Be

On Fire Island in the middle of the sea
I'm finally free—
On my own, the way it has to be
I can think, do and wear as I please
The walls come down for all to see
Not needing anyone to help me
Now it is I, where it used to be we
The mask replaced with hope imagery
Of unplacated love, truth and honesty
On Fire Island in the middle of the sea
I am finally free—
On my own, the way it has to be.

There is a mansion here, owned by Baron Rothschild
Full of jewels, lost loves—he seems quite wild
Yet there's a deep sadness in his eyes, amidst his style
I'm glad I am staying here awhile
I sleep in a loft, I snuggle—so I can't get caught
Health and true happiness can never be bought
He knows that from extravagant pain and pleasure
It's a kind heart—that's his true treasure

All our masks, may disintegrate here
We are who we are, there is nothing to fear
When tears are near—I remember
        my Wildflowers and Daisywishes
I remember the dreams my soul kisses
I look out at the strange wild sea
        Finally free—
On my own, the way it has to be.

The Soul of a Rose

Sunshine and rainbows

Silver star bursting

Like roses opening

To drink their fate—

Of beauty unsurpassed

In layers of softness

Feeling the sun

Breathing in the rain

Layer by layer of

      Wonderment—

      Unfolding—

Not one petal out of place

Never will there be anything

      So beautiful—

A perfect stillness of time

Burning beyond its fate—

      The Soul of a Rose.

Vulnerability

Strength derives from the insights we
    obtain when we are most vulnerable

It is only then, that the walls come down
    and the soul radiates through—

With honesty and impassioned
    abandonment

Our art can truly soar.

A Time of Sanity

Stress—Adrenaline Party
We're all invited
Meditation, Relaxation Techniques
Need more than a measly two weeks

Too loud, too bright, too fast
Take me away
To a simpler time
When we actually used our minds

Pantomime, dancing, charades
Playing pirates at sea
Or "Red Light, Green Light 1, 2, 3"
Our imaginations ran free

Time travel back
Is where I need to be
Reality or fantasy
Away from technology

Computer mind control
Replacing our creative soul
We must fit in, rather than "blend"
Is the message we send

Take a brilliant child today
Who sees the world in a different way
Of course! It must be ADD
Feed him Ritalin—our 20th Century candy

Rob his individuality and spirit
Trade his limitless imagination
For a standardized test score
Is at our school system's core

Yes take me away
Away from toxic crazies
Over-schedule my life
With a hefty dose of the lazies

I want to live, feel and soar
Not yearn for something more
Children and adults—one expectation shared
To grow and change with love and care

Respecting our inner timelines
Not bound by society's confines
To find strength, inspiration and completeness
In our imperfections and uniqueness

Learning comfort in silence
Without the clutter and noise
Listening to our soul inside
Happiness is ours to derive

Breathing in hope
Breathing in joy
Embracing what life could be
In a time of sanity.

How I Love the Way You Love Me

Feeling his love, beneath his stare—
One whole year…
Hearts thumping, trying not to care.
How I love that smile, his patience and honesty
My eyes melting within…
His heart, as he looked at me.

How I love the way you love me
Even if we never touch
You'll never know how much
Your trust, has opened me to love again.

In so many ways I'm still a child
Finally letting go of my controls—
My passion, drives me wild—
…Yet—I am scared of it
He knows that…
Riding my passion tenderly—
    with his eyes.

How I love the way you love me
Even if we never touch
You'll never know how much
Your trust, has opened me to love again.

We are now part of each other
Time is so precious—It flies by…
As we know no other—
He loves me for me and I for him
…With one voice.

How I love the way you love me
Even if we had never touched
You'll never know how much

42

Your trust, has opened me to
    love again.

Our Moment

I once had a purple balloon
Tied onto my wrist
By a dreamer—next to the
    carousel in Central Park—

His hands were shaking
So beautiful was the moment
Then all at once it loosened
To fly free—
        Soaring…

Towards the sun—
We watched it together
Till we couldn't see it anymore—

Not to disturb the moment
He immediately bought me
        a new one
Same color, a stronger knot
Trying to recapture, "our moment"

Desperately clinging to that moment
I kept the balloon till every
        inch dissipated
It seemed to last for weeks
Until it finally became a tiny
        rubber shell.

It's kept inside my "treasure box"
Alongside his poetry, music and
"other intensities" bestowed upon me.

There it shall remain
Though the carousel has vanished

Memories of this dreamer continue
To feed my soul—his soul—
        perfectly matched—

With a love so deep and
        <u>never</u> to be forgotten.

Sing a Solitary Song

Stop and Listen
Can you hear your voice?
Do you crave validation?
Is running always your choice?

Another relationship
Is that your answer?
Identity lost again
Being his private dancer

Just repeating patterns
No time to feel or deal
Leap off that crazy carousel
To finally process what's real

To hear the yearning
Deep within your soul
Your heart will soon reveal
What it needs to become whole

Trust your secret self
It will guide you far
Give yourself time
To process who you are

Seek your OWN approval
Make yourself strong
Look within your own eyes
Sing a solitary song

Give yourself permission
To embrace the unknown
As life's journey unfolds
You are now on your own

It's time to love yourself
Opening yet another door
For loving that special person
You were truly meant for.

My Life Begins and Ends With You

When I look into your eyes

I see mine

Within life's lows and highs

Our souls intertwined

As we realize there's more

Than just friends here

More for us in store

It's becoming so clear

Of what our lives could be

If we let each other in

So…break free with me

To risk is to win

With you by my side

Dreams CAN come true

Fears CAN finally subside

My life begins and ends…with you.

Truly Free

I wish there were words to explain how I feel

But love, you are the words that cause my soul to heal

I look at you now, in the morning light

The boy with the wild dancin' eyes has caused my soul

to take flight

By your side, the wind sings of danger on high

With gentleness and kindness our gypsy souls soar

the sky.

It's not approval from the masses we seek

For past misjudgments are only for the weak

After all, the pain then is part of the happiness now

As the cycle of life teaches us how—

—To forgive and to trust
—To live freely as we must
—To give back what is given
—To realize each precious day we are living.

It is only now that I finally see

That only with each other, we are truly free.

The Pirate & The Gypsy

For 11 years, we have retreated here
Its haunting, bucolic mystery always near
Weathered coastline renewing itself
       year by year
Its lovely familiar outline always to
         remain clear
For true souls to freely roam
Amongst this restless, evolving spirit
      we call home—
         Cape Cod

We are now called back to renew
       our vows
High atop a sand dune, it seems
       natural somehow
Surrounded by tall sea grass, wild roses
       ocean & setting sun
The Pirate & Gypsy came together
       again as one
As they always feel they can in this place
Their souls evolving without notion of
       time or space

We met by the sea,
On Fire Island, "Gay Paree"
You were a chef there
On your day off, without a care
I was writing by the shore
And there you were
Holding a bucket of clams
With your strong arms and hands
Blazing blue eyes a smiling
I decided to stay a while—

50

We danced amongst the cattails,
    surf and stars
Pirate & Gypsy, forgiving life's scars
For in those precious moments we
    were the perfect "blend"
Never questioning gifts the universe
    will send

Knowing full well this pirate
    shouldn't come ashore
I never asked for anything more
Bound for a fishing boat was
    his next port of call
Back to my singing career dreams and hospital
    work, I needed to stand tall

So we parted with an awkward laugh
    and lovely kiss
Both aware of feelings, hard to dismiss
As the ferry left the island, he yelled out to me
"I'll cook you a fantastic dinner soon, you'll see"
I watched his image intently, till I
    could see no more
Only that man in the moon, could foresee
    what was in store

Two months later, there was a knock
    at my door
A bunch of wildflowers and groceries
    perched upon my floor
Then suddenly my pirate appeared with
my kiss-stained letter, between his teeth
"Ready for that dinner?" I felt my
    knees go weak

My tiny kitchen transformed into a
        bustling café
A meal fit for a Gypsy Queen was
        created that day

We held each other all night—a
        delightful confection
As he marveled at my mask collection
Staring down upon us, from my ceiling
If only, he knew what I was feeling
Would this pirate come ashore?
Did I have the right to expect more?

Searching for work, he said he must do
As he made me breakfast—how time flew!
Another lovely kiss and on his way out
Will I see you again? I wanted to shout
He turned with a smile, and said would you please
Check the flowers on your piano keys
As I turned, I heard the door close
I tiptoed toward the piano and lo and behold
Were the flower stems threaded through
        his signet ring
How my heart wanted to sing!
Keep this ring close, his note did say
I would see him again, destiny's
        passion play

We've been together over 11 years now
The Pirate & Gypsy, city dwellers somehow
Cabaret shows, Off-Broadway, I've
        completed my CD
My pirate went back to school and
        is now an EMT

In every stage of life, a new
        focus becomes clear
Two souls unite and our beautiful
        son appears
He brightens every room with his
        creativity and smile
We look into those eyes, and know
        all is worthwhile
We try our best to give him all
        he needs
Living in the city, we have the
        opportunity to succeed

As much as we have to be grateful for
Deep inside, the Pirate & Gypsy
        yearn for something more
To sail, to sing, to create
        and explore
Renewing our vows here, opens that door

For the Pirate & Gypsy & their First Mate
        to freely roam
Amongst the restless evolving
        spirit we call home- -
        Cape Cod.

                With our Love,
                The Gypsy

My Baby Boy

Carefree he'll stay
My heart prays
As I watch him play
My Baby Boy

With sparkling eyes
How his heart flies
Weaving tales as he tries
To make them come true

As he grows, his destiny unsold
The world's wisdom yet to unfold
I try to teach him all I know
Slowly, gently holding—letting go

Finding life's keys in the highs and lows
How I love him so
My life…my soul

My Baby Boy

The Paths of Love

Enter the paths of love,

With its roaring tide and fragile heart.

Who takes it? Who knows it? Who feels it?

It was you all along, You remained

      within my soul.

Lost paths, paths of despair and memory

Joyful paths, paths of enlightenment and hope

Trembling and echoing with utter bewilderment

Then and now—

Paths of love, I will seek you

forever.

NEVER TO BE SILENCED

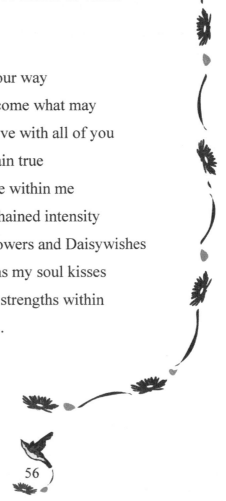

Feel it

Embrace it

Never Erase It

Don't be scared to feel and deal

Change the world by being real

Numbness silences the soul

Purpose, Compassion and Love makes us whole

As our journeys unwind

Our hearts intertwine

Embracing whatever comes our way

Amazed at the possibilities, come what may

Sharing this Gift of Perspective with all of you

Realizations unfold and remain true

The key has always been here within me

I have finally unlocked my chained intensity

I proudly reclaim my Wildflowers and Daisywishes

My vulnerability—the dreams my soul kisses

My voice, my blessing—my strengths within

NEVER to be **SILENCED**…

For Evil will **NEVER** win.

Renee Katz Music

never been gone

Renee Katz

Produced by: Christopher Marlowe and Renee Katz
TerraRose Records Inc.
Printed in the U.S.A. All Rights Reserved.
Photography: Nick Granito

1. **NEVER BEEN GONE** 4:01: {Carly Simon/J. Brackman} All rights administered by C'EST Music and Maya Prod. Ltd.-ASCAP

2. **ROMANCE OF THE CHILDREN** 3:49: {D. Friedman/ Z. Montgomery} All rights administered by Midder Music Inc.- ASCAP

3. **I COULD MARRY THE RAIN** 4:29: {P. Allen} All rights administered by Woolnough Music c/o Manatt Phelps Et. Al.-BMI

4. **JEEPERS CREEPERS** 2:29: {J. Mercer/H. Warren} All rights administered by Witmark M. and Sons –ASCAP

5. **I NEVER KNOW WHEN TO SAY WHEN** 5:34: From "Goldilocks" {L. Anderson/Kerr/J. Ford} All rights administered by Ankerford Music Corp.-ASCAP

6. **LEARN TO BE LONELY** 3:33: From "A Doll's Life" {L. Grossman/B.Comden and A. Green} All rights administered by Fiddleback Music Pub. Co.,Inc. c/o Warren Chappell Music Inc.-BMI and Revelation Music Pub. Co.-ASCAP

7. **MEADOWLARK** 5:16: From "The Baker's Wife" {S. Schwartz} All rights administered by Greydog Music –ASCAP

8. **RIBBONS DOWN MY BACK** 3:47: From " Hello Dolly" {J. Herman} All rights administered by Edwin H. Morris and Co.,Inc.- ASCAP

9. **SOMETHING YOU NEVER HAD BEFORE** 3:47: From "The Gay Life" {H. Dietz and A. Schwartz} All rights administered by Harms Inc. c/o Warner Brothers Inc.-ASCAP

10. **IT COULD HAPPEN TO YOU/ MY FOOLISH HEART** 5:12: {Van Heusen/Burke-Washington/Young} All rights administered by Famous Music Corp. and Warner Chappell Music respectively – ASCAP

11. **STRANGER TO THE RAIN** 3:33: From "Children of Eden" {S. Schwartz} All rights administered by Greydog Music –ASCAP

12. **EVERYTHING IS POSSIBLE** 3:40: From "Nefertiti" {D. Spangler and C. Gore} All rights administered by BMI

Total Time: 49:1

NEVER BEEN GONE

The wind is coming up strong and fast
And the moon is smiling on me;
Miles from nowhere, so small at last
In between the sky and the sea.

I'm bound for the island,
The tide is with me
I think I can make it by dawn.
It's night on the ocean,
I'm going home;
And it feels like I've never
I've never been gone.

Seagulls cry and the hills are green
And my friends are waiting for me.
Great ambition is all a dream
Let me drown my pride in the sea.

I'm bound for the island,
The tide is with me,
I think I can make it by dawn.

60

It's night on the ocean
I'm going home;
And it feels like I've never
I've never been gone.

I'm bound for the island,
The tide is with me,
I think I can make it by dawn.
It's night on the ocean
I'm going home;
And it feels like I've never
I've never been gone.

Oh it feels like I've never
I've never been gone.

ROMANCE OF THE CHILDREN

If I were the child that I used to be,
If I still had clouds for a bed;
I'd gather the stars that belonged to me
And custom a crown for your head.

I'd reach out my fingers and touch your face,
I'd wipe every tear from your eye;
I'd lavish a meadow of gold and lace
And, safe in my arms you would lie.

Romance of the children cannot be bought,
Romance of the children is free.
Romance of the children cannot be taught
But, you've given so much to me.

For now that I'm grown,
When I can't recall
Those times that were crystal and new;
I still can remember my childhood days
When I am surrounded by you.

For you are the times that are filled with song
And you are the children at play;

And you are the times that I thought were gone,
You chase all the sadness away.

You are all the love I could ever need,
You are all the joy life can give,
I still have the stars
From my childhood dreams
The crown for your head is still new.

And all of the love
That I've kept for years
I give, as my treasure, to you.

I COULD MARRY THE RAIN

I could marry the rain for doing my crying for me

I could marry champagne for when those old feelings bore me,

Marrying nighttime for hiding away is a good idea

But, the morning still comes

And those same old heartaches are here.

I could marry the spring if just for a new beginning

And need no wedding ring, just use a star

Then nothing gets to hurt you,

No one comes too close

When you love a thing like the rain or spring

When you love a thing from afar.

Then nothing gets to hurt you

No one comes too close

When you love a thing like the rain or spring

When you love a thing from afar.

I could marry the spring if just for a new, a new beginning

And need no wedding ring, just use a star

Then nothing gets to hurt you.

No one comes too close

When you love a thing like the rain or spring

When you love a thing from afar.

JEEPERS CREEPERS

Jeepers, creepers....where'd ya get those peepers?
Jeepers, creepers...where'd ya get those eyes?
Gosh oh, git up....how'd they get so lit up?
Gosh oh, git up....how'd they get that size?

Golly gee...when you turn those heaters on
Woe is me...got to put my cheaters on.

Jeepers, creepers....where'd ya get those peepers?
Oh, those weepers....how they hypnotize.

Golly gee…when you turn those heaters on
Woe is me…got to put my cheaters on.

Jcepers, crcepers....where'd ya get those peepers?
Oh, those weepers....how they hypnotize
Where'd ya get those…eyes?

I NEVER KNOW WHEN TO SAY WHEN

I knew on the day I met him,

He wasn't the man for me;

I knew I should just forget him,

But I had to stay and see.

Oh, I've been sad before;

And I've been mad before.

But, oh my friend, I won't pretend it was as bad before;

I should have told hard to stop and count ten;

Because I never know when to say when.

I know my way around,

I never play around,

Each time I fall I bet my all

He's gonna stay around;

It seems like everything is rosy and then

Somehow I never know when to say when.

But now I've learned my lesson,

And it's an easy one;

You gotta to keep them guessin',

Keep it fun, kiss and run.

The skies are stormy now,

My dreams all bore me now,

No candle lights, the lonely nights that lie before me now;

I swear it's done, it's done, it's over,

Amen!

Because again and again and again

I find I never know when to say when.

But now I've learned my lesson,

And it's an easy one;

You gotta to keep them guessin',

Keep it fun, kiss and run.

The skies are stormy now,

My dreams all bore me now,

No candle lights, the lonely nights that lie before me now;

I swear it's done, it's done, it's over,

Amen!

Because again and again and again

I find I never know when to say when,

I never know when, to say when.

67

LEARN TO BE LONELY

Make a new start, like a new chick

Scratching, fighting, cracking out of its egg

Shake your wet feathers dry, straighten that wobbly leg

Take a solitary stance, for a solitary dance, and learn to be lonely.

Make a new life, like a new star

Twinkling, sparkling, burning, glad to be born

Shine alone in the sky feeble, but not forlorn

Getting brighter every hour, to a million candle power and learn to be lonely.

Why do you need to search for a face to look into, to find your reflection?

The warm kisses that blanket the cold can't guarantee protection

Why be afraid to wake in the night with no head on the pillow beside you?

With no hand you can reach for to hold

Your secret self must guide you.

Use your time alone to grow strong, and discover the hidden being within you, all along.

Make a new you, like a new sun

68

Whirling, spinning, rolling free through the skies

Like a lone butterfly, open your wings and rise

Worse than being on your own, is to mate and feel alone.

You are your one and only

Learn to live,

Learn to be lonely.

MEADOWLARK

When I was a girl, I had a favorite story,

Of the meadowlark who lived where the rivers wind.

Her voice could match the angels' in its glory,

But she was blind;

The lark was blind.

The king of the rivers took her to his palace,

Where the walls were burnished bronze and golden braid,

And he fed her fruit and nuts from an ivory chalice and he prayed:

"Sing for me, my meadowlark

Sing for me of the silver morning.

Set me free, my meadowlark

And I'll buy you a priceless jewel,

And cloth of brocade and crewel,

And I'll love you for life if you will

Sing for me."

Then one day as the lark sang by the water,

The god of the sun heard her in his flight;

And her singing moved him so, he came and brought her

The gift of sight

He gave her sight.

And she opened her eyes to the shimmer and the splendor

Of this beautiful young god, so proud and strong.

And he said to her in a voice both rough and tender,

"Come along, fly with me, my meadowlark,

Fly with me on the silver morning.

Past the sea where the dolphins bark,

We will dance by the coral beaches,

Make a feast of the plums and peaches,

Just as far as your vision reaches,

Fly with me."

But the meadowlark said no,

For the old king loved her so,

She couldn't bear to hurt his pride.

Then the sun god flew away and when the king came down that day,

He found his meadowlark had died.

Every time I heard that part I cried.

And now I stand here, starry-eyed and stormy.

Oh, just when I thought my heart was finally numb,

A beautiful young man appears before me

Singing "Come

Oh, won't you come?"

And what can I do if finally for the first time

The one I'm burning for returns the glow?

If love has come at last it's picked the worst time;

Still I know

I've got to go.

Fly away, meadowlark.

Fly away to the silver morning.

If I stay, I'll grow to curse the dark,

So it's off where the days won't bind me

I know I leave wounds behind me,

But I won't let tomorrow find me

Back this way.

Before my past once again can find me,

Fly away.

And we won't wait to say goodbye,

My beautiful young man and I.

RIBBONS DOWN MY BACK

I'll be wearing ribbons down my back this summer;
Blue and green and streaming in the yellow sky
So if someone special comes my way this summer
He might notice me passing by.

And so I'll try to make it easier to find me
In the stillness of July;
Because a breeze might stir a rainbow up behind me
That might happen to catch the gentleman's eye.

And he might smile and take me by the hand
This summer
Making me recall how lovely love can be.

And so I will proudly wear
Ribbons down my back
Shining in my hair
That he might notice me.

And so I'll try to make it easier to find me
In the stillness of July;
Because a breeze might stir a rainbow up behind me
That might happen to catch the gentleman's eye.

73

And he might smile and take me by the hand

This summer

Making me recall how lovely life can be.

And so I will proudly wear

Ribbons down my back,

Shining in my hair

That he might notice me!

SOMETHING YOU NEVER HAD BEFORE

I've wondered what this moment would be like;
Pictured many a tryst here
Wondered what his girls would be like
And how many he's kissed here?

I don't care what all this is like
Little have I missed here
Oh my love
Listen to me now, my love.

You've had most everything but I know I bring to you
Something you never had before;
A kind of love that's deep and will keep forever new
Something you never had before.

You've had gay love before,
Come what may love before
You've had dancing, a waltz love
And false love before.

But now your life can start
For I bring a heart that's true
Something you never had before.

75

I know the art of keeping house
From a cellar to the dome.
But will this art be art enough
To keep this particular man at home?

I know the art of cookery.
He'll rave about my soufflé
But will this art be art enough
To keep him from drifting away?

And when we bid the world goodnight,
And together we climb the stair
Then will I have the art enough
The art that is needed there?
I want to be needed there.

A kind of love that's deep and will keep forever new
Something you've never had before.

You've had light love before;
For the night love before
You've had carefree, high-ho love
And no love before.

But now your life can start;

For I bring a heart that's true

Something you never had before.

IT COULD HAPPEN TO YOU/
MY FOOLISH HEART

Do you believe in charms and spells?

In mystic words, and magic wands, and wishing wells?

Don't look so wise,

Don't show your scorn,

Watch yourself

I warn you.

Hide your heart from sight, lock your dreams at night

It could happen to you.

Don't count stars or you might stumble

Someone drops a sigh and down you tumble.

Keep an eye on spring, run when church bells ring

It could happen to you.

All I did was wonder how your arms would be

And it happened to me.

The night is like a lovely tune.

Beware, my foolish heart

How white the ever constant moon

Take care, my foolish heart.

There's a line between love and fascination
That's hard to see on an evening such as this
For they both give the very same sensation
When you're lost in the magic of a kiss.

Your lips are much too close to mine,
Beware, my foolish heart,
But should our eager lips combine
Then let the fire start.

For this time, it isn't fascination
Or a dream that will fade and fall apart,
It's love, this time it's love, my foolish heart.

Keep an eye on spring, run when church bells ring;
It could happen to you.
All I did was wonder how your arms would be
And it happened to me.

STRANGER TO THE RAIN

Shed no tears for me

There'll be rain enough today;

I'm wishing you godspeed

As I wave you on your way.

This won't be the first time

I've stayed behind to face

The bitter consequences

Of an ancient fall from grace.

I'm a daughter of the race of Cain

But, I am not a stranger to the rain.

Orphan in the storm

That's a role I've played before;

I've learned not to tremble

When I hear the thunder roar.

I don't curse what I can't change

I just play the hand I'm dealt

When they lighten up the rations

I tighten up my belt.

I won't say I've never felt the pain

But, I am not a stranger to the rain.

And somewhere far from safety, there's a man who's walking free

His story isn't mine, but he's as much alone as me.

He has left his home to walk among the wounded and the slain.

And when the storm comes crashing on the plain

He will dance before the lightning to music sacred and profane.

Shed no tears for me,

Light no candle for my sake,

This journey I am making now

Is one we all must make.

Shoulder to the wind

I turn my face into the spray

And when the heavens open

Let the drops fall where they may.

If they finally wash away the stain,

From a daughter of the race of Cain

I am not a stranger to the rain.

Let it rain!

EVERYTHING IS POSSIBLE

I was blind and life was mere existence
Now behind my tidy little stance,
I can see the beauty in the distance and I want to dance,
I want to dance; you've given me the chance.

Thank you for the pulse that won't stop racing,
Thank you for the tremors of the knee,
Thank you for no ordinary morning.

Everything is beautiful and dangerous and possible
And, new to me.

The waves are not my enemies; the wind is now my friend
The road I hated yesterday; I never want to end.
I lift my eyes and everywhere the world is born anew
I see at last what's really there
But mostly, I see you.

Lift me to the very highest heaven.
Drop me in the great green boiling sea.
I am indestructible this morning
Everything is possible to me.

Let me have the lightning for my breakfast.

May my wildest nightmares all come true

Fear is irresistible this morning

Everything is dangerous; but you are here.

And fear is no disaster

I can face an unfamiliar shore

I was safe and comfort was my master

Suddenly I soar,

I never did before.

Everything is beautiful and dangerous and possible

And new to, new to, me.